Women In Mourning

Stories of grieving women.

by Jean Clayton

Illustrated by Mary McConnell

© 1996
All Rights Reserved
Centering Corporation

ISBN # 1-56123-094-4
SAN 298-1815

A Centering Corporation Resource

Centering Corporation
1531 N Saddle Creek Rd, Omaha NE 68104
Phone: 402-553-1200   Fax: 402-553-0507
EMail: J1200@aol.com

Contents   Page

Introduction

This book is for women and for those who seek insight into how and what women grieve. Because my own heritage is European and Christian, I can only dream of imagining the grief of women torn from a different culture, or women wounded by the grinding grief of the Holocaust, or women who are discriminated against because of race or religion. But there are many kinds of grief we share simply because we are women, some of which are not always recognized or supported. My hope is that you might find yourself somewhere in these stories and breathe a sigh of relief that you aren't alone, after all, and that your grief is legitimate and worth your most tender attention.

Grief is not new to women. Men die, and their wives weep, or cannot weep. There was Jackie Kennedy's shocked stillness in 1963, and more recently, Leah Rabin's tears, their husbands murdered, and the eyes of the world on their agony. We read of Queen Victoria, who, after the death of her consort, Albert, insisted that his dinner suit be laid out for him every evening. There are the women who journeyed westward with the wagon trains, noting in their diaries the many graves along the trail and weeping with those who wept and for their own dead. The book, *Children Die, Too*, begins with a drawing of a pioneer couple looking into the grave of a child, their capes billowing in the wind. Today, almost every newspaper lists the death of a child in the obituary column. And, although Scripture does not give women many active parts, it speaks often of the grief of women: Rachel, weeping for her children, the Marys sharing Jesus' agony at the foot of the cross, Martha railing heartbrokenly at Jesus because he did not arrive in time to save Lazarus from dying. Women know about grief.

Grief can lay us low. It can come from any direction, and it can roll over us like a steamroller. Yet we are the daughters and granddaughters of women who endured and survived the many loss-wounds of two world wars and the economic hardship of the Great Depression. Our mothers and grandmothers or their mothers have known the lonely losses of emigration. We all share their scars, but we also have the lodestar of their courage to follow. Women grieve, but somehow have always continued to nurse babies, hold down jobs, study, make birthday cakes, and hold the fabric of family and community life together. Each of us is the heroine of her own story, enduring and hoping.

A long time ago, I needed a way to understand for myself the tears that would not stop coming, the isolation, the thoughts of suicide. I remember being comforted to learn that my experience was not a special punishment but something universal, called *grief*. It was like finding a map while wandering in a strange country; it didn't immediately get me home, but I began to feel less lost.

I grieved the slow death of my marriage of twenty-two years. Earlier, our family had lived through a bungled adoption attempt which failed after sixteen months, with much pain for all of us.

There were many signs that Jason, the little boy we hoped to adopt, was abused and needed more help than we could offer but they were not recognized. Although it was the last thing I ever thought myself capable of, we unwillingly added to a small boy's history of rejection. He left us on a dreary November morning, and I closed the door behind him and began to cry. The tears did not stop for a long time, and the guilt remained with me for even longer. I cried in church, I cried in restaurants and supermarkets, I cried alone in my room.

I grieved, and my husband grieved — differently, just as couples grieve differently when a child dies. I wanted to talk and talk about what had happened, trying to make sense of it, trying to come to terms with this— to me — unthinkable failure of motherhood, and Bill did not want to talk about it at all, burying his feelings in his job. This added strain on an already fragile marriage was finally too much.

For a long time, I carried the grief of a mutilating illness in my teens. The pain began when I was eleven, just for part of each day, but I didn't know how to talk about it, because it was *down there*. I clamped my mouth shut like a good girl, going to school and coping with the many moves we made as a military family. By the time I was sixteen, the pain was unremitting, constant. I knew something was dreadfully wrong, but I still didn't know how to tell anyone about it. One night, I discovered a medical book with a description of my symptoms. They matched those of cancer of the bladder, and I read, in despair, that it was incurable.

In fearful, frozen grief, I prepared to die. Almost accidentally, in another hospital, my disease was finally diagnosed. Tuberculosis had eaten away an entire kidney and shrunk my bladder to a two-ounce capacity. Six months would have made the disease irreversible. I was seventeen. I spent the next two years in a hospital.

Eventually, my own journey led me into working as a grief counsellor. Because I know the road from my own travels through the deserts and mountains of grief and healing, I can share hope, even confidence, with those I meet.

I do not counsel only women. Men have their own struggle, but their personal and social context is different, and their ways of coping are also often different. Men are more likely to replace a lost partner within a year or two, and have more social and financial freedom. They are more likely to distract themselves from their pain by overwork or addictive substances. They also tend to receive more support from those around them (usually women) because women have tended to more easily extend nurturing. Sometimes, we do this to outrun our own pain by focusing on the need of others. Sometimes we do it because it brings us comfort. Sometimes we do it because we care.

The support we give is invaluable, and often the only kind available in a culture that no longer has symbolic mourning signs like black armbands, door wreaths or black veils to alert others to our need for special sensitivity.

Yet, we are not often skilled at being kind to ourselves. We frequently put our own needs last, as if that were a virtue. How nice it would be to end forever the myth that it is virtuous to always put others first! Far from being a virtue, surely it is irresponsible not to be kind to the one person for whom we are truly responsible. This self-support is especially important when the support of other women or society in general is not easily available to us.

We deserve to live...fully.

Grief is a process...
Not a neat, linear process, but a chaotic process, full of twists and turns. Still, we can make out three major phases:

Not True, The Great Angry Sadness and Moving On.

Not True: the feeling that the loss has not really happened, that it is all a terrible dream.

As in a nightmare, you struggle to wake up. You feel disoriented, distracted and fearful, and it is hard to think clearly, to concentrate or to remember. You wonder if you are still sane.

Then there is *The Great Angry Sadness.*

Irritability, waves of pain, and deep sadness shadow your days. You wonder how you can endure it, and whether it will ever end. *Moving On* comes with the hesitant slowness of spring after a long, bitter winter. It is not the forced moving on of Lot's wife, who was forbidden to look back and died of the accumulated salt of not crying, but the sure moving on of a river going where it needs to go and carving out new channels as it flows. It is two-steps-forward, one-step-back, but it still gets us where we need to go. We begin to notice that the present begins to occupy our thoughts a little more than the past, first with a good moment once in a while, then a half-hour, an hour, a day, until finally there is more peace than pain.

The grief process *is* the healing process. It begins with the question-with-no-answer, *Why me?* As healing comes closer, the question changes to *What now?*

It may take a long time, longer than family, friends, employers or society as a whole are willing to allow, and it is all right for it to take a long time because it just does. And yes, although the pain becomes less ferocious once the grief/healing process is entered into, loss leaves a scar, a place that will always be sensitive. In spite of the pain and the hurt and the tears, eventually we *Move on.*

Part One: Not True

There are some things too horrible, too frightening to face.
It is easier if we say, This Is Not True!

Cindy: A teenager loses her father
Cindy's father died one April afternoon in a freak electrical accident. She found out when she was called to the principal's office to be taken home. After the funeral, she received some counselling at school, and seemed to pick up the pieces of her life, going on to graduation and college. Following the breakup of a romantic relationship, she sought counselling and joined a grief support group. Cindy's healing began when, in the safety of the group, she revealed that she had been pretending to herself ever since her father's death that he was only away on a hunting trip, that it was *not true* that he had died.

****

Cindy and her mother fought constantly, though they had enjoyed a close relationship before the death of her father. Cindy was angry because her mother wanted to sell their house, and was thinking about dating again. As Cindy began to move out of her disbelief, a tiny bit at a time, she began to feel closer to her mother. Cindy's mother realized that the death was real. Her grief had not been delayed. As Cindy came to know her father had really died, that his death truly happened, her mother's reality was no longer a threat to her. Now, they could grieve together.

This first part of the grieving process is **protection**. But disbelief gradually wears off, so that we can once again handle the business of life, even though life may seem like something we are stuck with, rather than a gift. If the others around us are moving on in their grief and we remain back at the time the death occurred, relationship problems happen, and our own isolation can be torture.

Georgina: The grief of a grandmother
Georgina's favorite grandchild, three years old, died in a fall from the balcony of an apartment building. Georgina's family persuaded her doctor to put her on Valium after she was told of Cathy's death, to *protect* her from the awful truth. When I met her, she had just been taken off the drug, after six months. The reality of her grandchild's death was just beginning to hit her, and no one else in the family wanted to talk about it, saying that they had all moved on.

******

Tricking the body

Women who were tranquilized or given strong sleeping medication immediately following a death tell stories of having missed the funeral, even though they were present. Not being able to remember this important time makes healing that much harder. Although physicians seem to be getting away from treating grief as an illness, antidepressants and sleeping medication are still often used to "control" grief. Most women treated with such drugs declare that they do not like the feeling of unreality or hangover the drugs bring, and are uncomfortable about using them. Since medication is essentially meant to trick the body, it is small wonder that we feel something is wrong. Yet many of us feel powerless before our doctors. I can relate to that.

Just listen

Once, I had been hospitalized for a month following surgery, miles away from home and from my small son. I had always been a "good" patient, but when my treatment didn't seem to be working, I became very afraid. My yearning to be well again and to go home to my family overcame my need to be a perfect patient. My real feelings broke through. My surgeon ordered that I be given a sedative, and when the nurse arrived with the hypodermic, holding my arm as if I were a wild animal, I felt angry, alienated, and totally humiliated.

What I really needed was someone to sit with me, hold me, be with me, listening, until I had worked through my feelings. Later that evening, the surgeon came back to apologize. He knew, at some level, that the sedative had been a damaging way of dealing with my reaction. The feelings of grief on hearing bad news are intense and painful, but putting them to sleep is an unhelpful and temporary way of dealing with them.

To tell one's story and have it listened to in an accepting way, is the kindest, most useful possible response to grief. Medical caregivers cannot always change reality, but they do not have to make it worse.

Anne and Maria: Stillbirth Then and Now

When Anne's second child was stillborn, the delivery room crew dealt with it far differently than they would have done twenty years earlier, when Anne's mother endured the same experience. Then, Maria had quickly been *put under,* while her son's little body had been whisked away, forever. For months, Maria had stayed indoors, crying each day. For years, she looked at every little boy she met, thinking that her little boy (Sean, she called him secretly to herself), would have looked like that, at two, at five, at six. Maybe, she even thought, that *was* Sean. After all, perhaps he had been stolen, and wasn't dead at all. There had been no body, no funeral memories.

Things have changed. Anne was encouraged to hold her baby, and pictures were taken. A handprint, a footprint, a lock of hair. With her consent, a hospital chaplain had been called, to bless the baby and support the family. Maria had been called, and had brought the baptismal dress she had embroidered for her grandchild, to lay over the tiny body. When Anne was asked by the chaplain what name she had chosen for the baby, she just shook her head, unable to speak through her tears. But then her husband blurted out, Grace. *We'll call her Grace.* And then everyone cried.

The next morning, Anne asked for the chaplain. All night, she said, weeping, she had heard her baby crying. She asked if she could hold the baby one more time, just to be sure. The chaplain brought a big rocking chair from the nursery, and put it by Anne's bed. She called the morgue to tell them she needed the baby again, and would be right down. Stan, the morgue attendant, helped her wrap Grace's body in a soft blanket, and to put it into the small white wicker basket used on such occasions. She took little Grace's body back to Anne, who was sitting in the rocking chair, herself wrapped in a blanket, her face tight and wan. Carefully, the chaplain placed the baby in her mother's arms. Anne's husband sat in a visitor chair across the room, hunched forward, his face anxious and his hands tightly clasped. *My God,* said the expression on his face, *this can't be true.*

******

Anne asked her husband to press the call light after about an hour. He and Anne had been crying, but they sat closer together, and they were ready to think about funeral plans and Anne going home.

I cannot imagine a more painful experience for a woman than losing a child, at any age, except to be asked to pretend it didn't really happen. Or if it did, it didn't really matter. *After all,* many clumsily well-meaning people have said, *you can always have another,* as if human beings are interchangeable.

Not true, not true.

Anne knew her baby had died, yet she heard it crying. Many grieving women have sensory experiences of a person who has died, just as if it didn't happen, wasn't true. The head can know what it knows, but the heart has its own ideas. Women in mourning may smell the perfume or tobacco brand of the person who has died. My mother smelled the lilac cologne of her beloved grandmother years after she had died, and in one grief support group, three of the six people present had had a similar experience. Or they hear a characteristic footstep just outside the door, a crunching of snow — only it's August. One woman saw her sister, who had been buried a month before, in the wedding dress she hadn't lived long enough to wear. For about a minute, they gazed at each other across the bedroom, and then the vision - or whatever it was - faded away.

The women who shared these experiences were embarrassed. Each began with some version of, *You'll think I'm crazy, but...* As if love had nothing to do with the eyes, the senses, the heart, as if love does not inhabit us at all our levels, conscious and unconscious. Their experiences were out of the ordinary, just as dreams are out of the ordinary, but they were not crazy, not fluff.

When I saw the movie, *Superman,* and watched the hero's massive super-struggle to reverse the turning of the earth twenty-four hours, so that it would be yesterday again, and Lois Lane could live, I remember thinking that this grief is just like that. For years after my divorce I was sometimes seized by a powerful longing for yesterday, even though for the most part I felt I was moving forward with my life and accepting my new reality.

True, not true

If only this first part of grief were neatly fenced off by itself, and finished with early on! But it seems to be deeply intertwined with the later parts, crocheted into them just here and there with long, strong threads. It is one of the many surprises of grief, to think that we have left disbelief behind, only to find ourselves reaching for the telephone to call a lover who died several months ago, or finding our hearts bounding into our throats when, just ahead, we see someone who surely must be the one for whom our heart has been aching. One woman told me that when this happened to her she followed a strange man for several blocks, and had to speak to him to be sure that he wasn't her dead husband. It happens, that's all. It just happens.

Margo: Love and abandonment

Margo sat, shoulders hunched forward, a scarf covering her head, dark glasses over her eyes. She sighed often. She found it almost impossible to leave her house since her mother's death. Margo was torn by ambivalent feelings for a mother who had been wife to a violently alcoholic man, and who had eventually abandoned her children. Margo, the oldest, had been left to care for her siblings. Their mother had kept in touch just enough to keep alive the hope that she would one day return. Finally, after receiving a diagnosis of inoperable cancer, she had come home to die. Margo visited her faithfully in the hospital, spending night after night on the palliative care ward. She was shattered when her mother died suddenly while Margo was at home for a shower and change of clothes. Her guilt was immense. *I don't deserve to live,* she said over and over.

She had a fascination with sharp knives, which she would buy and give away as gifts, and told horrendous stories of abuse she had endured as a child. One night, her father, drunk, chased her mother and Margo with an axe. She said that later they used to laugh about this night. Margo's grief was so great, so deeply buried, that she began to cry, sobbing as if she were being torn apart. But the tears soon stopped; Margo saw to that. What she mostly spoke of was her despair, of how grey and meaningless the world appeared to her, of how she wished she could die, and would, if it weren't for her beloved son. Gerry was literally Margo's line to life, the one place she could see hope.

******

Grieving the loss of someone who has been abusive might seem almost unnecessary, beyond a *good riddance.* Actually, it is a formidable task, and survivors walk around and around their mixed feelings like a mountain of barbed wire.

Where do you begin the untangling, and how do you do it without bleeding?

Once in a while, the dark stories of harshness and deprivation lead eventually to good memories and shaky laughter. Sometimes it is only possible to lighten the darkness a little by talking about it, and even this is difficult, since abuse often includes a threat of punishment or death if a child tells, so that the very idea of telling can cause deep anxiety and guilt. How do you talk about grieving an abuser without revealing the abuse?

Grief and self-esteem
When you grieve, you are vulnerable. Vulnerability lowers self-esteem. Abused women often have very low self-esteem to begin with. The bruised self brushes off the abuse as not really important. Imagine not being horrified that you were chased by a drunken man with an axe when you were four years old!

Margo could not allow herself to feel anger towards her mother for abandoning her. It felt too risky, as if it might break the fragile connection that meant so much to her. Margo could only turn her negative feelings against herself. She often spoke of self-hate. She got some relief by looking after her brothers and sisters, who continued to turn to her for the mothering none of them had received.

Margo was a loving person. She recoiled in horror from the dark and agonizing thoughts and feelings that were part of her grief, and made a decision to stay with *not true.* Yet before she left she told me with a kind of cautious wonder about a miniature rose bush her mother had given her that continued to bloom, even though she could not bring herself to tend it.

Donna: Multiple loss
Donna looked dazed.
At seventy, she was trying to absorb the blows of several deaths in quick succession.

First her husband, to a heart attack,
a favorite brother, to stomach cancer,
a daughter, who died of breast cancer,
and finally a three month-old great-granddaughter to SIDS.

She would begin a sentence, then lose her train of thought, open her purse and close it, look at her watch, fidget in her chair. Her eyes seemed to focus on things no one else could see. Her religious faith had become meaningless to her, and she was on medication for anxiety. Sleeping was a problem. Donna said she kept busy, mostly shopping. She came for support at the urging of her daughter-in-law, who thought perhaps a group would help, people would understand how she was feeling. After less than half an hour, Donna said she had to be going, and spoke vaguely about coming back at some later date.

******

True? Not true?
Women grieving an abusive relationship may be reluctant to move out of disbelief because of the painful complexity of the task ahead, but women who have had many losses one after the other may feel dazed by their grief simply because there is so much of it. We become overwhelmed by so much difficult change, confused as to what is true and not true.

Barbara: Suicide and sobriety
Barbara was a recovered alcoholic with a horrendous history of tragedy and abuse. After the suicide of her lover, she was determined not to lose her sobriety. Mike's body had been badly decomposed by the time it had been found, and although he had been suicidal for some time, Barbara's torment was made worse because she and Michael had quarrelled at their last meeting and parted in anger. Barbara couldn't believe it.

******

When a death is sudden and violent, a murder or suicide, disbelief wraps us tightly in cotton wool so that we do not shatter. Within seconds, the whole landscape of life has changed. Hopes and dreams lie broken all around.

Numbing the pain
Barbara's temptation to numb her pain with alcohol was only slightly less than her determination to be sober. The tension was exhausting. Some women turn to TV watching, chain-smoking, binge-eating, shopping marathons, exercising or non-stop talking. They may try continual prayer or relentless good works. Anything to anesthetize the pain. But pain is always buried alive, and hides somewhere in mind or body, ready to burst out in disease or neurosis or anger.

Getting the pain out
At first, Barbara couldn't stop crying. Later, she paced the office, swore blue smoke, and waved her fists. Now she knew that this unthinkable thing was true, and she was outraged.

Anger is often the bridge from the island of disbelief to the wide main highway of grief, a fiery, fighting *NO!,* replacing the cold numbness of *Not True.* When it can be expressed in some safe way, it can help bring about healing. Once Barbara was able to feel again, she began to use the insights and skills she had learned through her twelve-step program to help her to work through her grief.

When anger remains disguised, when it is too deep for recognition, it can turn against the very person who has already been its victim for too long.

Theresa: An eight-year-old loses her mother
When Terry was eight, her mother died in the street of a heart attack. Terry's aunt moved in to help the family, and a year later married Terry's father. Very little was said about her mother's death. One day she was there, and the next she was gone. Everyone carried on as usual. Terry carried on, too, like a well-behaved little robot.

After Terry had grown up and become a nurse, her father was diagnosed with cancer. Terry, somewhere inside, decided that she would not let him die, and devoted herself untiringly to his care. Yet die he did. The day of the funeral, Terry saw, shockingly for the first time, the grave of her mother, since her father was to be laid by her side. After the funeral, she drove to a deserted place and took a massive overdose of medication. A will to live then helped her to drive to a hospital, where her life was saved, but afterwards, for a long time, Terry felt broken and ashamed. How could she, a nurse who cared for others, a person who valued self-control and logic, do such a thing?

******

Too much truth

Terry eventually forgave herself for her attempted suicide — or perhaps forgave the eight-year-old inside of her who was overwhelmed at last by a tidal wave of grief. The child part of Terry that had never known for sure that her mother was never coming back was finally faced with unquestionable evidence of her death. She had lost her father. Her mother was dead. She had failed.

A room full of teddy bears

There was something very little girl about Terry, a professional well into her thirties. She had an almost-lisp. She wore jumpers and embroidered blouses in pastel colors. Although she was happily married, she did not have children, but had a room full of teddy bears. It was as if in some ways her growth had been halted when she lost her mother, almost as if to show to the world that something terribly important had happened at eight years of age, and she was not going to let it be forgotten.

About *Not True*

Not True feels like: numbness, frozenness, a bad dream, confusion, fear, as if an avalanche were about to fall.

Not True looks like: bewilderment, smiles that don't reach the eyes, shocked stillness, aimless movement.

Not True is like an anesthetic our body provides to prevent pain from destroying us. It is meant to wear off gradually. It takes a long time to wear off completely.

Others can help by understanding this part of grief, and arranging to be there for us when the pain does hit.

We can help ourselves by self-care and gentleness, taking our time with decisions and putting support in place. We don't have to pretend we are fine when we're not. We can ask for help.

We help ourselves most when we do not contribute to the numbness with medication, addictive substances or over-activity.

Phase Two: The Great Angry Sadness
We rage, we weep. It is true.
This awful thing has happened and it has happened to me.

When *Not True* finally begins to melt away, the longest and sometimes the most painful part of the grief/healing process begins. Like feeling coming back into a frozen leg, it is agony.

The crisis may be over in terms of things to be done and arrangements to be made, but we are left with the consequences, the aloneness. People who supported us through the crisis drift back to their own lives, advising us as they go to get on with ours. We may nod, unhappily; we know it isn't as easy as that. We fear that things are getting worse, rather than better, especially if we were able to keep very busy during our *Not True* time. At least then there was some hope that we were only dreaming; now we know we are awake — and feeling.

Sad and mad
The main work, and it *is* work, of grief is sadness mixed with that old taboo, anger. Anger is a natural reaction when we feel robbed, betrayed, violated. It is empowering, giving us access to the rocket fuel we need to function, to make changes, to feel alive again. Yet we all know the adjectives for angry women: bitchy, aggressive, unfeminine, castrating. Most men fear anger in women, and most of us have grown up thinking of anger as wrong, rather than natural and useful.

When anger controls us
What we repress controls us, so that we *forget* to keep promises and appointments. Sour and spiteful remarks fall from our mouths like the snakes and frogs in the fairytale. Unconscious anger pushes us into driving too fast, to hurting ourselves. On my saddest days, I used to walk across busy streets without waiting for the light to change, almost hoping to be hit by a car. Dangerous in another way, anger that is not expressed can become the old grey shawl of depression.

Spitting it out
Obviously, it's not wise to hit others, or punch your fists through walls. Anger insists on expression, but it can be talked out, written out, exercised out. A tennis racket can hit a pillow. You can scream inside a car parked in a quiet place. One women rented a squash court for herself and hit out her anger. I used my anger as fuel for housework. I imagine many a floor owes its shine to a good head of steam!

The grief-garden
Mina, lost her husband to a sudden heart attack while they were on assignment in another country. Her grown daughters helped her move back home, where she led a very quiet life, on medication, for two years. Finally, she began to recognize that she was angry, but at first this gentle, middle-aged woman could think of no acceptable way to express it. Eventually, she hit upon gardening, assaulting the hard earth with her sharp spade. A beautiful garden eventually grew up, and we joked about the amount of manure it received.

Anger needs a focus
Sometimes the focus is the hospital, the doctor, the funeral home, a clergyperson. If professionals can allow themselves to be lightning rods, to hear complaints even when they are unfair, the anger often dissipates. Angry people don't always expect an irreversible situation to be fixed, but they do want their feelings to be taken seriously. Sometimes, anger is directed at the person who has died, sometimes at ourselves, as in why-didn't-I-take-better-care-of-him, and sometimes it is directed towards God, who can take it.

Pat: Loss and Anger at God
Pat was a gentle, soft-spoken nurse with a strong religious faith. When her father died suddenly, her faith was deeply shaken. She was disturbed by her feelings of anger at God, something she had never before imagined feeling. She was able to admit these feelings. The leader of Pat's support group grabbed a Bible, and turned to the Psalms. She read a Psalm of anger and lament, written two thousand years ago and still pulsing with energy. Pat looked tearful, and didn't say very much. The next week she returned with her own Psalm of lament, which she shared. She spoke of feeling relief, and peace.
*****
A crisis of faith
We somehow assume that women with a strong religious faith are automatically going to be sustained by it in grief. Yet to trust in a loving, protecting God and then experience abandonment and tragedy can cause a crisis of faith.

When a woman of faith is confronted with this spiritual crisis, she can either turn her back on her God, or she can have it out. Certainly no pat *God never gives us more than we can handle* formula (which is not in Scripture) can serve to bind up such important pain adequately.

Anger and the body

Even without the constraints of church teaching, many of us smile tightly through our anger, giving confusing double messages to everyone around us, and ourselves. But the body will not be fooled. If allowed, it will lead us into life. If allowed.

Nicole: Grief as stress

Nicole was grieving the sudden death of her lover. Nine years earlier, she had been though a divorce, and both her parents were dead. She was beautifully made up, fashionably dressed, and sat with her ankles crossed and to the side. She was talkative, and smiled when she spoke of her anger. She had Crohn's disease, a disease of the intestine. She attended one grief support meeting, then quit abruptly, unable to deal with the messy stories shared by the others in the group and not ready to become part of the sad and angry mess herself.

*****

The perfect enemy

Certain areas of the body are affected by stress more than others: the gut, the skin, the respiratory system. Grief is an acute form of stress. When it is repressed, our bodies work hard to call to our attention the anger and sadness we refuse to feel. These feelings may surface as a rash, or bunch up in the muscles of our necks and backs, or stiffen our joints. It is powerful energy, and it has to go somewhere and do something.

And how many of us, like Nicole, fall prey to perfectionism! My inner Fuhrer cracked the whip for years, making me controlling and critical of others, and saving the most exquisite torture for my image in the mirror. As much as I hated this destructive aspect of myself, it was shockingly clear to me that some hostaged corner of me secretly adored the perfectly pressed uniform and shiny jackboots. Only when I could admit this to myself could I allow myself to really enter the messy business of grief, with its runny mascara and swollen eyes, and to tolerate the frightening out-of-control feeling of anger.

*****

Isobel's grey sweater and slacks hung on her. She had lost thirty pounds in the three months since her husband's death at seventy, and she couldn't eat. She said she had a lump in her throat, but medical tests could find no evidence of it. One of the other women in the group befriended Isobel, and they would go out for dinner each week, just before the meeting. At the check-in which began each group, Isobel's eating progress would always be a topic of interest.

Isobel didn't say much at first, and what she did say was so softly spoken that it was hard to hear. She did not like it when others spoke of their anger, and denied feeling anger herself. Whenever the subject of journalling as a way to express feelings came up, Isobel would move restlessly. She did not like this idea, but one night, desperately unhappy, she grabbed her pen.. She couldn't put her feelings into sentences, but strongly and tearfully wrote **MAD MAD MAD MAD** all over a sheet of paper.

The next morning she called her lawyer and went "up one side of him and down the other" because she felt she hadn't been treated well. She called her doctor with some hard questions about her husband's treatment. That same day, a package arrived in the mail, addressed to her husband. It had arrived a month earlier, had been politely returned, and was from a publisher of romance novels. It contained a novel and two promotional wine glasses. This time, Isobel took a hammer and smashed the glasses into smithereens, and tore the book into many small pieces. She packaged the mess up neatly, with a cheque for the amount that had been requested, and returned it. And then she had lunch, because the lump in her throat had disappeared.

*****

Isobel's anger gathered itself into a lump in her throat, as if to threaten her very life if she did not find a way to voice it. When she wrote it in her journal, a connection was made. Isobel could begin to use her anger to effect change in her life.

Writing down the feelings
Journaling is often difficult in the beginning. I sometimes resist it, even though I know how much good it has done me. When I am in the grip of strong feelings that I do not know how to handle, I use journaling to loosen that grip. Sometimes all I can do is to write feeling words:
Angry. Disgusted. Hate feeling put down.
Want to kill.
Want to cry.

In my journal, I can be honest and uncensored and sloppy and free. Rather than stuffing my feelings into some dark place inside, as if I were ashamed of them, I honor them by writing them down. I keep my journals. I used to worry about my kids finding them after I died, but then decided it wouldn't hurt them to know their mother was a real person. They are my *herstory*. This is a page written on an angry, sad winter evening:

I feel grouchy and gassy and blocked. It made me angry to have so much mess around all weekend, even though I love the kids. I wanted some peace and quiet. Maybe it was the contrast of the retreat last weekend; that was such a blissful time. I get afraid. What if it's all over, and there are no more good times? But it is February, and even the bulbs beneath the earth are in the closest thing to death they know. Maybe they were afraid last fall, when I shoved them in a hole and covered them with earth. But life waits, knowing it is only winter sleep, and spring will come. Nothing is wrong. I want good things to happen because I need reassurance, and they only happen when it is time. Snow weighs me down, makes me feel heavy, afraid. I am forced to wait.

Journals are places for working through pain, as well as recording it so we can see where we have been. We come to terms with our situation, and sift it for its meaning. Sometimes, rereading it much later, we are astonished by our own wisdom...*Did I say that?*

Knock, knock
As a small girl, I sometimes felt that my hands were made of wood. I felt frightened, but I didn't know what to do about it. Certainly I could relate to poor Pinocchio's yearning to be real! Years later, I learned to recognize it as a warning that I was numbing out, going dead, and that there was something I wasn't allowing myself to feel.

Unpleasant sensations can be warnings, little pushes towards health and sanity, rather than signs of weakness pushing us towards worry or medication. There is a knotted feeling I get sometimes just below the back of my neck — I think of it as *The Claw*. It is my body's way of drawing my attention to tension; a comment, rather than a punishment. Our backs, necks and jaws are especially good at sending us such messages.

A dim grey place

When bad things happen, or "bad" thoughts or impulses arise, we may handle them by "going dead" in that part of our mind, memory or body. We may look alive on the outside, but inside there is this dim grey place of torture and phantoms, of not feeling. And then something happens that makes any amount of sadness or anger preferable to this hell, and all life breaks loose.

Kathy: Unfinished business and new life

Kathy began mourning after the breakup of a three-year relationship. She had also been divorced for six years.

Her childhood had been spent in and out of foster homes, and she had been molested when she was six. She had learned to be a very good girl indeed, to increase her chances of remaining at a foster home longer. When she married, her inability to communicate and deal usefully with anger had helped to bring down her marriage like a house of cards, but she found a job and tried to rebuild her life. The relationship she found was with an exploitive man who had taken full advantage of her compliance, but when it collapsed, the pain had been too much to bear. All the old, numbed pain had come beating at the door of her heart, clamoring for expression and recognition.

*****

A new great angry sadness will bring old pain to the surface: all the incomplete angry sadnesses. There is a part of us that craves wholeness, completeness, that claims happiness as a birthright, and seeks to spew out that which poisons us. Kathy, at mid-life, was in a place rich with possibilities, ready to work with the unclaimed parts of herself. She joined a women's assertiveness group, to learn ways of coping with conflict. There she met another client of mine and they became fast friends. A door opened which led to a whole hall of other doors. Kathy had the courage to begin and continue the process.

Thanks, but no thanks

When a grief issue is explored, a woman may see that it is one of many strands in a web, that the time is ripe for a reassessment of many things. And sometimes women will stop the process then and there, because they see it could lead to large changes in their lives and relationships for which they are not ready.

Maria: Unfinished business and old pain
Maria was a teacher who experienced the sudden death of one of her students. Left to face the student's mother, Maria was at her wit's end, not knowing what to do or say. It became clear that Maria had unresolved issues in her own life. Long ago, she had miscarried her only pregnancy. She had been raised to bite the bullet, and endured her tragedy stoically. Now her pain was awake. As Maria sifted through the years and her relationships, she became uneasy, as if she were tiptoeing too close to the edge of a dangerous place.

*****

When pain wakes up
Coming face to face with a woman who had lost a child awoke Maria's pain for her lost child, and her doomed hopes of ever being a mother or grandmother. She had not had the support or the experience to mourn her losses.

Miscarriage
Women who miscarry are among the most neglected grievers. There is an element of shame that complicates things, as if the baby is *lost* through carelessness, as one would lose a purse, as if the woman has failed a crucial test. It is a lonely grief, heart and body deprived together. Even if there were mixed feelings about the pregnancy (aren't there always?), it is a lonely grief. Sometimes the urge to bear a child is so powerful that women will put themselves at risk again and again.

Elaine had miscarried eight times. Each time, she set her teeth and became pregnant again. Finally, she gave birth to a little daughter prematurely, and spent most of the day and night in the neo-natal intensive care unit, brooding ferociously over her intubated little girl. I smile, remembering her triumph when she was at last able to take this little girl home with her, and my awe at her courage.

Grieving an abortion
Abortion is another subject loaded with emotion, including grief. How could it be otherwise? We are dealing with birth and death together, the most primal of issues.

Liz: A sad, angry choice
Liz was in her early forties. She had borne her children, ages two and three, late. When she became pregnant again, genetic testing revealed abnormalities that were potentially life-threatening. Liz's husband insisted that the pregnancy be terminated.

He saw no reason for the family to go any further with this development. Liz complied, not sure that she could handle it herself. She went alone to the hospital, while Rick cared for the children. She was deeply ashamed of having an abortion, and could not bring herself to ask anyone else to accompany her. A counsellor spoke with her before the abortion, a compassionate woman who had seen many women through this crisis. Liz went ahead, and was sent home in a taxi a few hours later. Rick didn't want to talk about what had happened, then or later. Liz wanted to talk about it all the time. Their relationship became so rocky that Rick threatened to leave. Liz then sought counselling outside the marriage; she had to talk some more.

*****

Liz's situation was tragic. Through no fault of her own, she had been impaled on the horns of a reproductive dilemma, and did not have any genuine choices about its resolution. Fearful and unsupported, she had agreed to an abortion which was not her choice, but that of her husband. She felt she had betrayed her unborn child, her church and herself, and suffered agonies of guilty *what-ifs* , torturing herself with questions for which there were just no answers.

Liz's situation was especially difficult, but many women who decide on abortion feel backed into this painful choice by circumstance. They do not do it gladly, but because they see no other way, and they do it in pain and with grief, and often they must do it alone.

Conception is a huge event in the life of a woman, and when the pregnancy ends, however that happens, she bleeds everywhere. There is no contradiction between acknowledging this and claiming to be deeply feminist. Feminist poets have expressed this pain eloquently, as in these lines by Eileen Moeller in her poem written ten years ago:

little tadpole
gone back to the ghostworld
I went to the crossroads
could go no further
could go no further
left you fine as a mustache hair
on your father's soft lipped mouth
saying no
ten years ago
I bled on a white padded table
and the crone sang her black song

and here I am now
still carrying you
a question mark curled asleep
in the keening dark of my mouth
a seed unspoken
you rise
pearl in the moon of my thumbnail
tiny mirror

I am still bleeding

Phantom pregnancy

Once I was called to comfort a woman who had been happily expecting her second child, only to be told that there was no child there. Her body had played a cruel trick on her, and had developed a molar pregnancy, complete with hormonal changes (because a placenta develops, although there is no baby) and swollen abdomen. We looked at one another, bewildered. She felt tricked, humiliated, foolish. Fortunately, these are relatively rare, but unfortunately this means that there is little support for women who endure them.

No easy answers

Sometimes it is suggested that adoption is the answer to unwanted pregnancy. It can indeed be a good answer. Both my daughters are adopted, and all of us are deeply grateful to their mothers. But such a gift is not without pain.

I have no way of knowing what the birthmothers of my daughters have suffered, whether they long for their children or what it has been like to live with their choice. And now that I am a grandmother, I wonder about the pain their mothers felt when this baby disappeared forever from their lives.

I do know that in spite of all my love, my daughters sometimes grieve for their birthmothers and wonder why they gave them up. I have no way of easing their pain, and can only be with them in it. I also know from my experience with Jason that adoption is not always the answer. There are no easy answers.

Marilyn: Single motherhood

It wasn't easy for Marilyn to tell her mother she was pregnant. Joel was her first real boyfriend. She was nineteen and she was sure he loved her, but he was still in school. Marilyn's mother was divorced and had tried hard to raise her daughters well. Marilyn knew she would blame herself, and she did. After her first angry reaction, she gave Marilyn her full support. Marilyn wanted to keep the baby, and she wanted to continue to live at home until Joel finished school in three years. The pregnancy was a difficult one, but eventually Marilyn gave birth to a healthy boy, three weeks prematurely. Marilyn's mother and Joel were with her in the delivery room. Marilyn held the baby out to her mother, but her mother motioned to Joel, who reverently took his son into his arms. One of the nurses nodded approvingly; this was not such a bad beginning.

****

Where is the grief in this story?

Little things, at first, like noticing the wedding bands on the other women in the ward, and feeling as if she should be ashamed rather than proud, like them. Like being given few clothes and gifts for her son, receiving no congratulatory bouquets of flowers, except the one from her mother and sister. Like having the social worker come around the next morning to ask personal questions, and having to answer them because Marilyn knew she couldn't make it without government assistance. She held her son close, fiercely resolving to somehow make their future together a good one.

The long sad hours

During the first months of her son's life, Marilyn stayed in bed most of the day, getting up just before her mother arrived home from work. Only later did she share her depression with her mother. To her, *But why didn't you tell me?* Marilyn replied, *I didn't want you to think I couldn't handle it.*

Marilyn's depression might have been eased with medication, but what if she had needed instead those long solitary hours of sad low-energy to reflect on her losses and her future? Marilyn was grieving the loss of her freedom, the loss of her dream of bringing her baby proudly into her own home, of having a husband to turn to for support and assistance, of having a life of her own before becoming a mother.

Mixed feelings

Marilyn's mother grieved, too. Although she welcomed her grand-child, she felt judged, along with her daughter, and anxious about the future. And she felt hurt when a colleague mentioned, unasked, that he knew a couple who would be glad to adopt Marilyn's baby, if she decided to give it up. When her small house began to fill up with baby equipment, she felt torn between a desire to provide a nurturing, welcoming environment and a longing for the order, peace and quiet that had been so important to her. Yet she grew to love her grandson deeply, and felt hurt rage whenever she thought she detected judg-ment or condescension in the way he and his mother were treated.

Mothers alone

Marilyn did have two important kinds of support that many women must somehow do without; the support of her partner and the support of her parent. One of the most chilling stories I know of is about an eighteen-year-old who had been thrown out by her parents. She was literally homeless, and raised her son in parks and bars, making a few dollars as a prostitute. The woman who told me this story was the grown daughter of this little boy, who not surprisingly grew up to be a very abusive man. And then there is Mary Oliver's poem, *Strawberry Moon,* telling the story of a great-aunt who, impregnated and aban-doned, climbed into the attic, and stayed there for forty years, because *It was considered a solution/ more proper than shame/ showing itself to the village.* The ending of the poem is wonderful:

Now the women are gathering
in smoke-filled rooms,
rough as politicians,
scrappy as club fighters.
And should anyone be surprised

if sometimes, when the white moon rises,
women want to lash out
with a cutting edge?

Much that makes the grief of women different from that of men has to do with our role as birth-giver and still, for the most part, child-raiser. A widow with small children must not only care for herself, but for her grieving children. Sometimes it can feel good to be diverted from your grief by the busy-ness of childcare, but sometimes the strain of not being able to just go away alone makes it harder. Add to that the demands of a career, and the pressure is tremendous.

Sandy: Widowed with children

Sandy was widowed at thirty-two. One weekend her husband had been drinking coffee with her at the kitchen table, and by the following weekend he was gone. Forever. Monday had been spent in the emergency facility of the nearest hospital with Sam struggling to get his breath after a massive heart attack. By Friday the funeral was all over. That sudden, that unbelievable. Now Sandy sat at the table, four-year-old Lynnie leaning against her knee, thumb in her mouth. William, seven months old, was taking his morning nap. Sandy wanted to cry and cry, all alone, but she had to *be strong* for the children. She had just returned to work after a long maternity leave, and could take a week of her vacation to find childcare. Up till now, she had been able to work out a system of shared responsibility with Sam. Sandy felt as if she were made of glass, bloodless and brittle and cold. The future no longer beckoned, friendly and familiar. It had become malevolent and strange, another planet, and she was on it, all alone.

*****

And the world goes on...

A woman in mourning once remarked that loneliness is a feeling, but isolation is a place, a place where survivors suddenly find themselves, all alone. They can see the sun shining and their neighbors leaving for vacation. The mail arrives, the newspaper is delivered, but they are all alone, shifted to another dimension. It is a crazy-making experience, like having the world turn upside-down, only no one else seems to have noticed it. The sky has fallen, and everyone else just carries on as if nothing has happened.

In mourning at work

In the middle of this disorientation, this isolation and paralysis, women like Sandy have overwhelming demands on their resources. They must somehow balance a job, care for their home and children and attend to their own needs. They are stretched as never before. Like many women, I found comfort in having a job to go to where I was required to concentrate for a few hours each day on something besides grief, but for months I cried all the way home in the car.

For a time, we may feel less competent than usual, but if the workplace is at all supportive to grieving employees, there can be a kind of relief in work. If an employer and colleagues are unsympathetic and distancing to grievers, then work can be toxic, an additional stressor.

Mothering grieving children
Small children can be a bittersweet bridge between the old good life and the unchosen new reality. While there can be comfort in the warm little bodies and in being needed, there is the added pain of living daily with the grief of children, seeing and hearing their suffering and not being able to *fix it* for them.

The memory book
Lynnie reverted to thumb-sucking and bed-wetting, going backwards through her small store of experience to find a time when life was more secure, and Sandy found that it helped to have a third person deal with some of Lynnie's questions and fears. The counselor suggested that Lynnie and Sandy put together a memory book, using a photo album with plastic-covered pages. Mother and daughter used this as a focus for their grief, recording memories of Sam for later in life. Sandy sought support for herself, eventually taking one evening each week for time alone or with friends.

Time and Work
Women often ask anxiously if it is true that time will heal their pain. And it does...to some extent, and with work. One of our natural processes is healing. If we cut ourselves, healing kicks in almost immediately. If we break our hearts, in some way, and maybe a little crookedly, that heart tries to make itself whole again. If we speak of our pain to supportive people, and cry when we need to, and are kind to ourselves, we can help our healing along.

Healing is not forgetting
When we grieve we sometimes fear healing will mean forgetting, the ultimate betrayal.

As women we are valued for our ability to care. The loving heart of the mother, the loyalty of the daughter, the faithfulness of the wife are praised in Scripture, and family stories. I have a large silver spoon my grandmother gave my mother when she made her one trip from England to visit us. She was a proper lady with very little money, and Mother is fairly certain Grandmother swiped that spoon on the boat, to have a gift to bring. Grandmother was heartbroken when we moved to Canada, and I have dim memories of my own protesting three-year-old grief on leaving her house, where I had lived since birth. My spoon reminds me of our shared love and grief, and of her courage in leaving her tiny village to travel three thousand miles to visit us.

How do we move on in our own lives after a loss? When is it all right to move on? This is often the subtle, unspoken dilemma that feeds prolonged grieving. How much grieving is enough? In cultures where a woman is burned on her husband's funeral pyre, at least the message is clear...a woman's life is over when her husband dies.

The feeling of failing
There may also be the implication that a woman is to blame when her husband dies. Even if he eats too much, drinks too much, and refuses to go to the doctor when he has pain.

Sandy blamed herself for her husband's death. She *should have taken better care* of him. She knew it wasn't logical, but that was how she felt. She also felt a lot of anger at what felt like desertion, because the truth was that if he had taken better care of himself, he might still be alive.

Ivy: Widowed at Seventy-nine
Sometimes Ivy jokes that her husband died the death of his dreams, on the golf course. Ivy is an amazing woman, a seventy-nine year old with the slight figure of a teenager and the energy of one, too . Church work, volunteer work and her family fill her days. But because they love Ivy, her family, her minister and her doctor all urged her to seek grief counseling. She was a little too busy, and they were worried about her. Ivy and Carl had enjoyed a long, loving marriage, and the busy-ness was clearly a way to distract, to make the remaining days of her life endurable. What did she want? She wanted to talk about Carl and their life together and the dreadfulness of life without him. But it distressed her family to see her in pain, so Ivy made jokes.

******

Loneliness
Like me — perhaps like most of us — Ivy found it hard to share her pain with her children. They were in pain, and her deep, old instinct was to protect them. I used to come home from work after my divorce and go straight upstairs to shower. I could cry in the shower without anyone knowing. I kept busy at work during the day, but the pain seemed to make a fresh assault as soon as I left the building. I was one clean mother, let me tell you. And one lonely one.

Women miss the physical satisfactions of marriage when a partner dies, having someone to snuggle up to in bed or just to touch — at any age. Sometimes regular massage can bring comfort.

Loving women
Some women enter into relationships with other women to meet the human need to touch, to feel connected. If they are not blatant about it, society often turns a blind eye to same-sex affectional relationships between older women.

When women lose a same-sex partner, grief can be made more painful by not having their grief validated by others. Women who are open about their affectional preference are more likely to have lesbian friends for support, but may still not experience compassion from family members or others in their lives. We pay a lonely price for loving outside the lines drawn by our culture.

The friendship factor
Women grieve not only husbands and children and lovers, but friends, brothers, sisters, parents. People to whom they opened their hearts, cried with, exchanged nurturing and encouragement and letters and phone calls and little gifts. And laughed with. We always remember the laughter. For some women, a sister was this beloved person; for some, it was a friend. And for some, it was a mother. A very old mother.

Ellen: Grieving a beloved — and old — mother
Ellen was seventy-two years old, and grieving the death of her ninety-six year old mother in a nursing home. She was angry and hurt by the reactions everyone had to her grief. She was sick of hearing about her mother's long life and of the expectation that Ellen must have known her mother would die one of these days and therefore shouldn't be sad. *We all have to go sometime,* they said wisely, not knowing how Ellen longed to punch them in the face. Ellen's mother was her best friend. They understood one another, and enjoyed one another's company in a special way.
*****
Ellen found comfort in sharing her memories of her mother. Later, she found herself able to return to the nursing home where her mother had lived to do volunteer work with some of her mother's friends.

My mother, my friend
Many women grieve deeply the death of a mother long after they have left home. Often because Mother was also a friend. Women grieve because Mother won't be there to see her grandchildren grow up, graduate, marry — to advise, assist, or to just chew things over.

A daughter grieves because her mother won't be there to go shopping, to take to lunch or to give Mother's Day cards. When the movie *Little Women* came out, I was touched to see the theater crowded with little groups of women, women in their thirties with their little girls, and seniors with their middle-aged daughters. Yes, friendship in a relationship is deeply important. It's absence becomes painfully clear when a relationship is severed by death, intensifying our grief.

Grieving what wasn't

Sometimes women feel embarrassed about grieving strongly for a parent, arguing that no one can change the past. True, but we can alter the way it affects us in the present, can go some way towards de-clawing it, de-fanging it. We can at least work towards forgiving ourselves for feeling pain and longing for what will never be, and perhaps learn a little about mothering ourselves. With help and the courage to explore our own depths, we might even be able to attain the peace of forgiving our mothers for what they couldn't give us.

Toni: The Forgiveness Connection

Toni had been in therapy for two years after her husband died. She withdrew when hurt rather than working through the problem with the other person. One day Toni told how angry she became with her mother because of her refusal to discuss anything difficult. *She just pretends nothing is happening, Toni* railed. *I feel so shut out, so far away from her.* The therapist looked at Toni in silence, and then Toni made the connection. Her way of handling conflict had been well learned. Some of her problems with intimacy began to come clear. *Oh, God, when I withdraw its because I feel hurt, as if I can't let anyone see me in pain. And if that's why my mother does it....* For the first time, Toni felt connected to her mother in her sadness.

******

The wounds of war

Toni's mother was a war bride. She married her husband in the highly-charged atmosphere of wartime England. When the war was over she left her own country, like thousands of other young women, very often with small children, for that of her husband. Every week, thin blue airmail letters flew back and forth between Toni's mother and her mother. Only twice had there been enough money for visits to take place between the mothers. Sometimes Toni would find her mother at the kitchen table crying, with a letter in her hand. She would always be brusque at these times, embarrassed and angry to be caught in her grief, even by her own daughter.

Strangers in a strange land

My own mother was a war bride. After the war, she was sent from England to live in Montreal with her husband's mother who was angry because her son had run away to join the army and was less than welcoming. In an alien country, with no family support, my mother and thousands of women like her had only each other. Strong friendships grew between them whenever they found each other. For women who ended up on isolated farms, even this consolation was denied.

Married strangers

Although unions of this kind were sometimes successful, many husbands were almost strangers to their wives and had been through trauma. Yanked out of ordinary life into war, they had experienced deaths and maimings of new friends. They may have had to kill or wound others, and then live with that knowledge without debriefing or support. Depression, alcoholism and withdrawal were often the legacy of their experience, and became part of the hasty bond of their marriage. Some marriages survived. Some did not, grief upon grief.

War creates other wounds, too. And other kinds of courage.

Fannie: Pain is always buried alive

Fannie is in her eighties, almost blind. She is in a wheelchair and nabs passersbys to engage in conversation. She tells stories of wartime England whenever anyone will listen, though she has often been told to *forget it, put it behind you.* It is all still alive to her, unfinished business. She tells of having nothing to feed her children, or her soldier husband, of riding her bicycle for miles to find a garden to raid for turnips, of begging a store owner for leftover cheese. She tells of the terror of nights in air-raid shelters, tries to describe the sound (which still is in her ears) when a young parachutist plunged to his death yards away from her one night. She tells of twice emerging from such shelters to find her house burned to the ground. Not once, but twice. Her love for her family and her creativity also are told - the special occasion when, to celebrate, she crumpled red cellophane and put it in the fireplace, and it was *almost as good as a real fire*!

If Fannie is moved to a different room in the nursing home where she lives, she becomes extremely upset. Losing a home, even a shared room, is a painful echo of those mornings when she emerged from the underground stuffiness of an air-raid shelter to gaze upon the smoking blackness that had been her home.

Fannie gets impatient about needing to dwell on her past, accusing herself of self-pity when the sad-angry days come. She is slightly comforted by knowing that she is dealing with unfinished business. Each telling of each story may deal only with a molecule of her pain, but still it does nibble away at it. Her pain has not frozen her zest for living. Best of all, her social impulse, her desire for connectedness, is still strong. Each time she tells her stories, I am reminded that courage and grief go hand in hand, and that healing can continue indefinitely when the griever is willing and able to share her story.

Lara: Loss of a breast

Lara, at forty-five, had returned to work after the wedding of her only daughter. She was enjoying her professional achievements and her colleagues. Suddenly, after her annual mammogram, the room was full of earnest, concerned caregivers, including her own doctor. Lara had a lump in her breast needing further tests immediately. Surgery was tentatively scheduled within the month. Lara felt paralyzed with fear and grief, but could not bring herself to share these feelings with her friends. *Fine. I'm fine,* she said. In the hospital, after a radical mastectomy, she asked her family to keep visitors away. After her release Lara refused to answer the phone, using the answering machine to screen all calls. She tried to respond to the concern of a few close friends, going through the motions but unable to relate with welcome or warmth. Friends wondered whether she might prefer to be left alone, and their calls grew further and further apart and eventually stopped entirely.

Lara had always found anger difficult to express. She had reason to be angry — test results had been mixed up at a time when her breast might have been saved. Never very sure of her attractiveness, Lara now felt deformed, ugly. Why should she be the one to suffer like this? Was it a punishment for finally beginning to move towards personal success, rather than giving all her interest and energy to her family? She knew that didn't make sense, but that's what it felt like. And why should her friends continue to bounce along with two healthy breasts? Where did they get the nerve to expect her to continue as if nothing had happened to her, to carry on an ordinary conversation? She felt rage at everyone, and then felt guilty about her rage. No one understood. And she couldn't bring herself to explain. *Fine. I'm fine,* said Lara silently to herself, tears running down her face.

******

Words are not the most important part of communication. Tone of voice, timing, eye contact, touch, are what we listen to with our deepest hearing, just as we did when we were babies, and had not yet learned the other language of words. Lara knew she wasn't fine, and her friends knew it too. *I'm fine,* translated as *Keep away, don't touch me.* Lara used it like a shield and her friends respected her, yet felt helpless to offer comfort. And I could relate.

One of the legacies of my tuberculosis was an ileal conduit, an external bladder which requires me to wear a rubber bag cemented to my body over a small opening on my abdomen. After my operation the pain was not well controlled, and this showed in my face. A psychiatrist came to the unit looking for another patient who had taken an overdose of drugs. He mistook me for her, probably because of my devastated facial expression, and I was terribly humiliated. Why? Because I didn't want anyone to know how I felt.

At that time patient support services were few and far between and no one came to talk to me about how it felt to be a young woman facing a lifetime of rubber bags. My defense was to be a good patient, cheerful, accepting. After the psychiatrist's mistake I made sure no one else could see my pain, even though I dreamed regularly that I was changing my bag in the bathroom and would look up to see all the neighbors watching in horrified fascination. It was a long time before I could tell anyone what the surgery had done to me or meant. I felt I couldn't talk about what had happened to me. I withdrew or was careful to keep the conversation intellectual. I sabotaged intimacy and unintentionally courted loneliness. My children remember me during this time as an uptight mother, the last thing I wanted to be.

I felt that by keeping my anger and pain to myself, what had happened to me couldn't affect anyone else. But grief is too powerful an energy for one person to contain. It overflows.

Who could I have told? Who wanted to hear about this fearful thing? Lara felt this strongly. She imagined friends backing away, covering their breasts, making some invisible sign to ward off the evil eye of cancer. Now, twenty-five years later, if I could find no friend willing to listen, I would seek professional help. There is healing in hearing, in sitting in respectful silence, unflinchingly offering loving friendship, in looking *It could be me* right in the eye and refusing to look away.

The Mothers: Loss of a child

Wilma's son died at 21; in jail, by his own hand. She brings pictures of him with family members. Again and again she speaks of his good qualities, aware of the facts of his incarceration, but needing to balance these with her mother-memories of him as a baby, of his first day at school, of him running in the house, red-cheeked, on a winter's day. There was more, she seems to be saying. There was more. He was my little boy, my son. Let me tell you the rest of the story.

Janey's little girl died of leukemia at age nine. Janey is tortured by memories of her inability to take away her daughter's pain. Somewhere inside she is convinced that she should have been able to do that as part of her parental covenant. She remembers staying with her in the hospital until the child could fall sleep. One night, exhausted, Janey tiptoed down the corridor after an evening of storytelling and lullabies only to meet the resident assigned to her daughter. He was coming to do an examination, to awaken Janey's little girl again. Janey can't forgive herself for allowing him to do this, or for at least not going back to the room with him. She was just so tired. It is hard now for Janey to take time for herself, as if flogging herself would somehow make it up to her dead child.

Lila found her baby boy dead in his crib one morning. He was three months old. No one could give her a reason why he died. Lila speaks of an ache inside that will not go away. It is always there, but it hurts most when well-meaning people tell her how much worse it would be *if she had really gotten to know him.* Bone of her bone, born in her heart and carried below it; how could she have known him any better? His room is just as it was. She feels that some day she may be able to dispose of his belongings. But not yet.

Together the mothers cry, "How could this happen? How could God let it happen?" They speak of guilt, of wanting to hide in their houses, of the many insensitive comments of those who have not walked this Via Dolorosa.

******

Empty arms
There is the pain of not being able to bear a child at all. Shopping trips are made late at night, when you are less likely to bump into mothers pushing strollers. Thousands of dollars are spent at infertility clinics, which put stress and strain on a love relationship. The devastation of the scarlet stain accuses you of failure.

Living with disability
There is the pain of bearing a disabled child; the bewilderment, the disappointment, the guilt, the curtailing of personal freedom, financial drain. Perhaps less often considered, is the pain of *being* one.

Angela
Angela is nineteen and was born with spina bifida, a spinal lesion which results in some paralysis to the body below the lesion. Angie is able to walk on her own, even though all her life she has been teased by her peers about walking "like a penguin". She doesn't mind that as much as she minds not having any control over her sphincter muscles. She has to wear pads for incontinence and a diaper at night. She learned to catheterize herself when she was four. She isn't tall, has a pretty face and a winning personality. Because her birth-mother was alcoholic, she has learning disabilities. These make it hard for her to understand how money works or how to *think like other people.* Angie attends a special school. It is co-ed and some of her friends are interested in dating and talk of marrying someday. Angie knows it would not be a good idea for her to get pregnant because it would be very hard on her body and her baby could also have spina bifida. Besides, she knows it is not likely she will ever be able to live on her own. Sometimes she gets angry and sad. When she feels overwhelmed, she tries to talk with her adoptive mother or a friend, or writes in her journal. Sometimes she talks to a social worker. She tries to live one day at a time, and is often quite happy.
******

Just as I am
Angela, like all of us, longs for the ordinary bliss of life - a lover, a home of her own, perhaps marriage and children. She isn't likely to have these things. It isn't fair, but that's the way it is. She is entitled to be accepted as she is, even celebrated for her loving nature, her musical ability, her sense of humor. She is also entitled to grieve, to have her moods, and to seek relief in daydreaming. Her mother grieves, too, for Angela's pain. She worries privately about Angela's future, sometimes very secretly wishing they could die together when the time

comes, as a way to banish the specter of Angela in an institution. Although she could never do it, she understands very well why some mothers take the life of a disabled child, and it is not for themselves. Her grief is a long and patient pain. Grief is a crisis, a long, slow crisis.

Ongoing grief
Angela's grief is ongoing, requiring continual adjustment. Losing a relationship not to death but to another person or circumstances is an ongoing grief, and means seeing the other person again and again to discuss legal affairs or children. Some couples can achieve good, civilized closure. Some can become friends again. Others find each meeting full of pain and resentment that hasn't been worked through, a pain that spills over onto children or into the new lives they are trying to create and live.

Is divorce a legitimate cause for grief? It certainly bears all the marks of grief — guilt, shame, anger, fear — and sadness.

Jean: My own divorce
As a young woman, I was very judgmental about divorce, especially where there were children. I thought that marriages were stuck together with willpower and love. I thought that if the love grew smaller, the willpower could grow greater and compensate. I thought that I was capable of any amount of sacrifice for my children. When my marriage began to be barren and lonely, when no amount of effort seemed to bring about any change, I gritted my teeth. I said to myself that I would just keep going, one day after another; then I would die and it wouldn't hurt any more. I didn't realize that nothing just stays the same; it gets better or it gets worse. It got worse. I finally sought counselling, but there wasn't much to be had in our small city. I made an appointment for six months down the road and by the time that six months had passed, I was long gone. Deeply ashamed, I found a job in another city and moved there with my daughters and one son, who rejoined his father with my blessing after six months. My other son stayed in the city where his friends and life were.

I don't know where the courage came from to make this move. I had no idea how to use a bank machine, I could barely put gas in the car. I rented an ugly little house next to a vacant lot where a few years earlier a house had blown up in a natural gas explosion, a piece of information that made all of us quite nervous!

Over the next several years, I worked hard to reconcile with my children, who were sad and angry. I did my share of getting into foolish, defeating relationships until I decided that I liked being single, and until I learned how to handle it.

When the children's father remarried I helped my daughters dress for his wedding. Although Bill and I had been civil before his marriage, we struggled with jealousy and misunderstanding, and were not able to discuss these feelings in any helpful way. After all, why should we suddenly be able to communicate when we had not been able to before?

******

Alone and afraid

Of all the stories of divorce-grief I have heard, I share my own because I know it best and because I hear its themes again and again. If you have been there you know that I was relatively fortunate. Many women find themselves suddenly deserted without knowing why. I at least had the advantage of knowing what was happening to me. Many women find themselves without money; I had a job. Many women lose their children in the courts or find that the fathers of their children disappear, never or seldom to be seen again. Mine paid support, and kept in touch with his children. These things made the work of grief easier, but it was still long and slow.

Re-inventing our lives

The work of healing from grief forces us to re-invent our lives by ourselves. It is deep change, hard, dirty work, and we are sore all over at times... birth at its most mysterious.

The image of rebirth is a spiritual one, and grief is a spiritual journey, transformative and profound. Nor are women whose whole frame of reference is spiritual — women in religious community — immune from a kind of divorce.

Lois: Leaving religious community

Just before the changes in the Catholic Church known as Vatican II, Lois joined the order of nuns who had been her teachers all through school. She was eighteen, the oldest of a large and devout family. Her parents were proud of her decision, unaware that Lois was in her heart seeking refuge from a world with which she did not know how to deal, from peer pressures and confusion she felt about sexuality. Supported by the order, she went to university and became a school librarian. But after nineteen years, Lois became deeply depressed. One of her dearest friends in the order left, and it felt to Lois as if her life had lost its meaning. She began to face many fears. Greatest was the fear of growing old in the order, of never knowing independence. In tears, and after much reflection, she asked to be released from the order. Lacking any experience of life on her own, Lois had many fears about her future and the ordinary business of living. She worried about being homeless, and wondered if she would end up on the street, sleeping over a heated grate like some people she had seen. She was relieved to learn that the order would turn back to her the money she had saved during her years as a librarian, and would help her to find a place to live. Telling her family and her friends in her community was an ordeal Lois somehow managed. Looking back, it seemed to her as if she never stopped crying during that time. And even though she is a gifted woman who later enjoyed considerable professional and personal success, sometimes on special feast days, remembering the community gatherings she loved, she cries again.

******

Women like Lois are not as numerous as the Jeans, but many of their experiences are similar, especially around practical issues like managing money. As for the tears, well, we all know about the tears!

Gradual grief

Circumstances that cause women grief are not always dramatic. Sometimes, it sneaks up on us — like chronic illness. Many women struggle with chronic illness such as multiple sclerosis, lupus, fibromyalgia, or chronic fatigue syndrome. There are differences between these conditions, and there are many shared kinds of loss.

Megan: Chronic illness

Megan is thirty-two, married, with children ages four, six and nine. She doesn't like to complain and has always been proud of her supermom status, but when months of doctor's visits resulted in a diagnosis of fibromyalgia and chronic fatigue syndrome she was forced to face the fact that her life had to change radically. Because she continues to look well, she finds the thinly-veiled skepticism of some of her family and friends hard to bear. Forced to resign her job because of her lack of energy and inability to concentrate, she fights depression. Her children don't always understand that she is no longer able to take part in many of their activities, and she feels like a failure because she can no longer keep her home immaculate or even keep up with the laundry. Some days she has more energy than others and struggles not to try to make up for lost time, knowing it will lead to greater exhaustion. Gradually, Megan is learning to pace herself and enlist the help of her family. She attends support groups and gets some comfort from being with others who admit to being angry and sad because of their illness and — best of all — realize that it *is* an illness.

Suddenly old

Imagine being young one day and old the next! Women with chronic illness have to deal with limitations that age imposes on the rest of us gradually. They move slowly, rest more often, need more sleep, suffer from insomnia. They find it hard to concentrate or even remember why they put the kettle on. They are forced into a kind of retirement while their friends continue to be active, yet without the white hair and wrinkles that make slowing down understandable to the rest of the world. They may be considered lazy, may have to seek a disability pension, or be judged uninterested parents when they do not show up for every school activity. Medications, along with their enforced inactivity, may cause them to gain weight. And needless to say, their love life takes a nose dive. They have a lot to mourn.

The rose garden

At a series of workshops for women with chronic illness, we used the analogy of having been forced off the main highway of living into a rose garden — which can be a very prickly place. We took a good look at some of the longest thorns, all the kinds of loss, identifying such things as loss of freedom, friends, career, health. After we had spent a long time looking at the thorns, we looked around to see if there were indeed any roses. We laughed to realize that there was a different kind of freedom and new friends, but most of all there was relief that the loss reactions they had been feeling were normal and shared by others. They were in mourning and were entitled to grieve.

What do you know that you didn't know before?

In the movie *Camelot,* King Arthur, played by Richard Harris, is facing the crumbling of his world. He goes into the forest where he played as a boy, seeking wisdom from his old teacher, Merlin. Merlin's uncanny eyes look at him with compassion. They help him travel in imagination high in the sky as a hawk, deep into a forest pool as a fish to see the world differently. When he returns, Merlin asks, *What do you know as a hawk that you didn't know as a man?* And that is the question, *What do you know as a woman with a chronic disease that you didn't know as a healthy woman?* Therein lies much wisdom.

That is like the question asked on the path that leads grieving women, ever so slowly, from The Great Angry Sadness into Moving On. What do we know as women who have grieved, who have descended deeply into darkness, that we didn't know when the sun shone? What do we know about ourselves, our strengths, our gifts, our worth as individuals, which no catastrophe can take away?

About The Great Angry Sadness

*Anger and sadness come in waves.
Take a breath, and try to let them roll over you until they pass.

* Find safe places and safe people for your grief. Share it with those not likely to make it worse by preaching or spiritualizing it, people who will just let you talk. A support group can be helpful.

* Give yourself lots of time. It takes as long as it takes.

* Give yourself a break from grieving once in a while. It is okay to laugh or go out socially.

* It is also okay not to go out socially - you don't have to do anything right now, and you don't have to explain. *No, thank you* is a complete sentence.

* Anticipate your needs. If it will be an especially rough day — appointments with a lawyer, arrangements with the cemetery, a birthday or anniversary, give yourself the evening off. Early bed after a bubble bath, with a cup of tea and a juicy novel can work wonders.

* Look after your health. You are fragile right now.

* Plan something to look forward to in the future.

* Whenever possible, minimize stress. Buy ready-made food or eat out, send a card instead of a letter, let some of your chores go or pay someone else to do them occasionally.

* Read stories of others who have been through what you are experiencing. If you can't relate, choose another book.

* Journal. Write letters to the person you are missing. Give them hell, or write them poetry. Write it down, get it out.

Phase Three: Moving On
Then there comes a time when we are once again
interested in life. We re-invent ourselves. We move on.

The *what do we know?* question is only heard when we are well into healing. Before that, we just don't care! But a transformative experience like grief does bring change. How else could it be? Our world has changed, as well as our feelings about how life works, or doesn't work. We change to fit into our new life.

Sorting through
Sometimes we are urged to *let go*. Some women find this helpful. I have found it about as useful as *relax* while I am white-knuckling the dentist's chair. I feel better about *sorting through* grief, keeping what feels good to me, shelving what I might want to look at later, and trying to keep my hands open to any good gifts the future might have.

Composting
My other favorite image for a creative way to deal with the past is to compost it, rather than to try to bury it alive or to wrestle with it as an enemy. Composting it means digging it into the earth of our experience to enrich it. However much rubble there may be in the ground of our past, it is our ground.

As without, so within.

Although grief and healing take place within, our actions in the outside world can help us to understand where we are in the process.

Adele: Inner and outer transformation
Adele felt embarrassed because she was still mourning her husband's death eleven years earlier. She was mourning their unhappy life together. There was abuse in her marriage, as well as in her childhood. She had two daughters and bent over backwards to make up to them their own difficult childhoods. They manipulated her in every possible way. She still had trouble saying *no* to her daughters, who continued to be demanding as adults. Adele learned to define and hold her boundaries. She began to respect her own needs. Her little house would be perfect *if it had a stronger front door and a nice big window in front.* Adele decided that she would use her savings to bring about this transformation of her house. She was delighted by the way the change reflected her own moving on. The nice strong door reminded her and told the world of her new ability to say *no*, and the *nice big window* symboled her brighter outlook on life.

Shrining

We create our lives as we go along. An unwillingness to change a room in any way after a death is one type of shrine. Sometimes grieving people seem to be waiting for the dead person to return, so great is their pain, so strong their feeling of *not true*. The nursery of a stillborn child can be preserved for years, but the effect is as though there is a little cemetery in the house, casting a pall over any further life. It is a way of saying. I *wish I had died, too. I did die.* Certainly it can feel as though part of us did die. One mother put a picture of her son, who was killed, on a table. Near it was a small box of his precious things. A silk flower lay on top of the box. It was a tiny shrine people could look at, visit, but not be forced to stay there.

Wait just a while

The opposite reaction, immediately discarding everything that belonged to the dead perso, can also be destructive, especially if it is done by others to *help* the bereaved person,. The painful sorting process is necessary at some point to healing, but each of us is entitled to her own unique timing around this process. Some tackle it sooner than others. Some prefer to do it alone, others in company.

Goodbye, house...thanks!

Saying goodbye to a place can also help us to move on. After my divorce, when I learned my home in another city had been sold I went alone one day to say goodbye to it. I caught the new family moving in. They kindly allowed me to go through the house. Not all the memories were happy, and not all were sad. I cried and my visit helped me to realize the finality of what had happened, just as seeing the body of someone who has died brings home the fact of the death.

Every so often I still go by that house to look at it. It still draws me, nine years later. And I accept that in myself I don't need to be perfectly healed. I don't need perfection in anything, I need life. And ninety-five perfect of perfectly healed is a lot of life. Healing does not mean forgetting, and partial moving on is still moving on.

Sarah's Baby: Grief takes as long as it takes
As a chaplain I was often with mothers whose unborn baby had died. My memory of my first time is especially clear, standing in the hall with a young couple in tears while the mother waited to be taken for delivery. Afterwards I spent time in the quiet room with several of the family, all women. They gathered around the baby, her purplish little body dressed and bundled in a blanket, tearfully exclaiming over her resemblance in various ways to the mother or the father, almost as though the expected happy occasion had occurred. But quickly the admiration turned to expressions of grief and they moved back from the baby as if the ritual had been choreographed. Then together, we did the blessing I had been asked to do, with the maternal grandmother holding the baby, and all of us in tears.

About a year later I heard my name called excitedly and turned to see the same young father. He told me that he and his wife had just become parents of a healthy child. Sarah was lying with her baby in her arms, and we admired him together, but soon she was in tears. My visit, along with the fatigue of giving birth, had brought back in a flood the memory of her loss a year ago.

******

No other baby
Losses can take a long time to heal, even a little. I thought of the many mothers who had told me how frustrating it was to be told by well-wishers that they *could always have another baby.* That may be true, but it is always irrelevant. Sarah's tears proved each baby has its own permanent place in the heart of its mother, and is irreplaceable.

A sign of hope
Sarah's tears told us the new baby was not a replacement for the first, but was instead a sign of hope. Sarah and her husband had decided to move on with the flow of life rather than anchoring themselves at that place in time where their first baby had died.

Women in mourning show other signs that they are beginning to move on — a new hairdo, brighter clothes, new make-up and jewelry. Women speak of being able to watch videos of special times or look through picture albums and of either being able to tolerate photos of the beloved on display, or of being able to put away such things. One woman told me with clearly mixed feelings that she didn't always notice a picture of her dead husband anymore, a picture with which she had in the beginning held comforting, nightly conversations.

Pictures are powerful
Photos evoke lots of feeling. I have always been the family photographer and after my divorce it was years before I could look through my albums without deep feelings of sadness and regret. Gradually the pain lessened. Now I find myself beginning to hang family pictures in places where I will see them often, and doing it with pleasure.

The taste of grief
Food is something else loaded with emotional connections. For the first year on my own I found it impossible to cook meals that had been family favorites. The rich smells, seeing the spattered pages of my favorite cookbooks; even shopping for the ingredients were just too difficult. I wanted to start all over, creating new meals that would only have associations with my new life. And I did this until I had experienced enough healing to begin to try the old recipes again. Now I cook them regularly and happily and they have associations of my new life, as well as the old. Moving on means that we have a chance to gather new memories, not replace the old, but to gently shove them over so that they don't take up all of our attention any more.

Celebrating in mourning
If you have been anywhere along the thorny path of grief, you know about the pain of special times: anniversaries, birthdays, Christmas, Hanukkah become mazes of confusion and danger...how to get through them?

In spite of feeling that we might like to just sleep through these days, it is usually not an option. Others often depend on us to find some creative way of observing them. You may prefer to do everything just as it has always been done, and derive comfort from feeling you have been able to maintain tradition. Or it may help to acknowledge the great change in your life by changing your celebration, reinventing tradition.

Using ritual to help
Women sometimes wonder whether they should risk upsetting others by speaking of the person who is missing at such family times, or increase their own loneliness by pretending not to be thinking of him or her. Sometimes a ritual acknowledging the change can help. A ritual is a way of connecting powerful feelings to everyday life, using simple materials. When it is shared with others, it increases closeness rather than increasing loneliness. For example, on a special occasion a

picture of the beloved missing person on a little table with a rose or a candle nearby tells others that the loss and grief are not forbidden subjects. Sometimes women hesitate to do something like this for fear of reminding others of their grief, but grief is usually like the proverbial elephant on the coffee table that secretly has the attention of everyone in the room anyway. And how can you remind someone of something when they are thinking of it constantly? Yes, there may be tears, but there will also be relief.

Noreen and Jill: Creating ritual to assist change
When Noreen was seven years old her mother died in an accident, leaving Noreen and Noreen's three-year-old sister, Jill.

Jill had been slow to talk, and when her mother died she stopped altogether for two years. Noreen eased her grief by concentrating on Jill and interpreting her needs to her father. He remarried within a year, and life seemed to go on. Noreen eventually had a daughter of her own. When Noreen turned thirty, the age at which her mother had died, she became very preoccupied with her mother's death. She took comfort in learning that the chaos she was feeling was normal. Even so, she could hardly wait to turn thirty-one, feeling as if death was lying in wait to snatch her when she reached her mother's age. It even felt as though her mother and death were waiting together. She needed her mother to finally die, and stay dead. She began to work on creating a ritual that would permit her to move on alone.

On the weekend following her thirty-first birthday, Noreen, Jill, and Noreen's little daughter, Carol, drove out of the city to a deserted beach. They made a circle of large stones, and then they decorated the stones with Queen Anne's Lace and wildflowers, a circle of life and death together. Sitting within the circle they talked of their mother and grandmother, cried, and said goodbye. When they drove back to the city, they said they felt a hundred pounds lighter.
******

Catching up
As Noreen told me of their ritual, I noticed how animated her expression was. Before, she had appeared dreamy, as if hypnotised by the past. Time seems to stop when a great loss occurs. For a long time it is as if we are lost in the past, preoccupied with it, and we have to run to catch up with the rest of the world which has moved on. As we heal we can give our attention more and more to what is happening *now,* in the present moment.

Creating healing

Noreen was an artist and later held a showing of a series of pieces she had created during this time. Some of them were small and patched in places with bandages, symbolizing both her memories of her mother as a nurse and Noreen's own healing process, as well as Noreen's child-eye view of her world at this time. Earlier she had been unable to take herself seriously as an artist, although she had been affirmed by others and had been able to sell her work.

Another woman, Amy, was musically gifted. She knew she was moving on when she wanted to sing again and was able to join a choral society. Sometimes she cried as she sang, but she sang.

When energy returns

Whether your talent is art, music, writing, crafts, fashion, baking, sculpting, decorating or anything else, it takes energy to create and, in grief, our energy is elsewhere. Mourning is hard work. We know we are moving on when we begin to feel enthusiastic about the activities we enjoyed before our loss.

Convalescing

Moving on is like the return of health after a long illness. We begin to sit up and notice our surroundings and what is happening. Our appetite returns. We notice the seasons again. Sleep comes more easily. We begin to think that we might want to go back to work, or to take up a piece of needlework that we laid aside for a time. We still cry, but not as often.

How long does it take? Days, months, years. It takes as long as it takes. Noreen reached a time when it felt right for her to look at the impact of her mother's death. It was not the first time she had tried to deal with it. Children re-grieve with each step in development. As adults, we enter new emotional territory as we develop, having, as it were, new cards to shuffle into the deck of our understanding of life and death.

Shame and mourning

It is not an easy thing to trust another with pain. If the cause of our pain seems shameful to us, then it is even harder.

Terry Returns: risk and new life

Remember Terry? She overdosed when overwhelmed by the pain of seeing her mother's grave for the first time. For months Terry was so ashamed of her suicide attempt that she avoided even her closest friends. She went to another city for counselling, so she wouldn't run into anyone she knew. She shopped in another city, wearing sunglasses, so she wouldn't be recognized. She couldn't bring herself to return to work. Finally she took a night shift at the hospital. At first she felt awkward and shy, but gradually realized that she was not being judged and that people were very glad to have her with them, which was healing in itself.

******

Grief and the workplace

Terry had options about returning to work; not every woman does. She also had the luxury of congenial coworkers and an understanding supervisor. More than one woman has left her job because her grief was not tolerated by her colleagues. The values of the workplace — efficiency, speed, order — are not always friendly to the messy reality of grief. Very few days are allowed off, though an understanding employer may extend this by granting a leave of absence or vacation time or sick time can sometimes be used. Ask for help.

Opening the subject

Because most of us are reluctant to pry into the feelings of another, the woman in mourning often needs to be the one to initiate conversation about her situation. We may assume that no one wants to know or that no one remembers or cares about the person who has died, or whatever loss it is we are dealing with, but often others are waiting for us to open the subject. Choose your support carefully. Other women who have themselves experienced loss are most likely to understand how you feel.

We are not alone

We are often so careful to keep our troubles to ourselves, imagining that everyone else copes so much better. Once Terry was able to be open with her colleagues about her suicide attempt, they felt more free to tell her of their bad times. Terry was amazed to discover how many other women knew what it was like to feel abandoned and overwhelmed. She was also glad to realize that she had become more compassionate towards patients who were struggling with grief and depression. She had become a better nurse.

Last gift

Going through grief and healing can leave us with greater compassion and bigger hearts. Sometimes I think of that as the last gift of the beloved dead. Our comfortable views of life crumble, but in their stead is greater wisdom. Most self-help and other-help movements are begun by people who have *been there*. Although we don't want to hear about this when we are grieving it is a sign that we are moving on when such thoughts begin to have the ring of truth.

Carla: The Pony in the Manure

When Carla was forty-two her husband went to his native country to sell some property. While there, he had a heart attack and died. Carla had to go and make funeral arrangements in a foreign country. After her return to North America she had to sell her husband's business and care for her four children. Although she had been very active in her church she found it hard to attend at all. She and Leo had been leaders of a very active couples group in the parish. Everywhere she looked she was reminded of her loss, yet she could not visit her husband's grave to talk to him, something she felt a great need to do. And because her children had not been able to say goodbye to their father, or even to see his grave, they had great difficulty grieving.

Carla had lost not only her life companion but her own identity as a leader within her community. She had enjoyed being someone to whom others turned for wisdom, and this role was not easily available to her as a woman alone in her ethnic community. Eventually Carla joined a bereavement support group, not only for support but to observe how such a group was run. She asked for extra reading material so she could learn to run such groups for the other widows within her tightly-knit parish community. Carla regained some of her old confidence as she took on this new role, and although she still grieved for a long time, she was able to do it with other women who understood, giving help and receiving it at the same time.

******

Perhaps you have heard the story of the little girl who wanted a pony for Christmas, and on Christmas morning ran to the barn. She saw only a huge pile of manure. After a moment shr took up a shovel and began to work away at it. When asked what she was doing she said, *Well, with all this manure, there must be a pony in there somewhere!* Maybe that's as good an illustration as any of the courage and hope of women in mourning. Carla found a gift in her pile of manure, and took it back to share with other grieving women.

Cobwebs on the shovel

What happens when the shovel gathers cobwebs in a corner, when it just seems too heavy ever to lift up? I think of a woman who has become bitter and cynical. I think of one who refuses to leave her house at all. I think of another who is in danger of losing a job she really values because she can't bring herself to return to work. And there are many, many women who became physically and seriously ill following a loss which they handled by pretending it didn't happen — including myself.

Yet it is never too late to begin this life-giving process. Two steps forward....

You've met Ivy, whose husband died playing golf. Although beautiful golf days are especially painful for Ivy, and though she says the process is very much two steps forward and one step back, at eighty she has begun to do volunteer work for the blind, arranging for rides to appointments. She also shares her computer skills with patients in a long-term hospital, and is active in her parish. She arranged for a tree to be planted in her husband's memory, along a walkway they used to enjoy. There is a plaque on the ground at the base of the tree and she often drops by to say hello.

Dorothy's book of life

And there is Dorothy. Her husband was dying a long slow death in a palliative care unit. They were simple people from a farm near a small town. While her husband slept Dorothy sat by his side, writing in a school notebook. After he died she returned to the unit to give each of the staff a copy of a little grey book. She had written Sam's life story and had copies made for everyone who had cared for Sam in his illness. It opened with his birth and contained many descriptions of the weather and the names of all his teachers, as well as the everyday drama of their marriage and family life. It closed with a description of his funeral.

What stays with me is the memory of the peaceful expression on Dorothy's face. Sam was dead, and she knew that, but she had found a way to make sure none of us would forget the hard-working man she had loved. She was in mourning, but not to stay.

Thanks...for the memories

Finally, there is the moving-on I know best, my own. It has been a long time since my divorce, almost ten years. For most of that time I felt stuck in angry, sad, powerless feelings whenever I had to have contact with my former husband.

Generally I functioned well, but when Bill called the kids or came by to pick them up my stress level would go up and my self-esteem would go down. Only recently, after much hard work in therapy, was I able to look Bill in the eye and stay centered. I saw that he was getting older, and no doubt he was thinking the same about me. We had a civil, almost friendly conversation, which I initiated. What astonished me, though, was my impulse (not acted upon) to throw my arms around him and hug him — not because I was still in love with him, but because there had been things I loved about him. It wasn't longing for the past, but rather a tribute to my own healing.

I could feel more than anger and sadness.
I could remember — and feel — what had been good between us.

I had moved on, and I gave thanks.

About Moving On

* Grief and healing can and may be revisited many times before the process is completed.
    This is not failure, it is just how we are made.

* Try to be open to what others have found helpful, but find your way...what helps you.

* Respect your process.
    Don't shove it or push it faster than it can go.

* Accept partial healing, partial forgiveness.
    Perfection has no place in grief — or in living fully.

* Your painful initiation has made you a card-carrying member of a great sisterhood of courageous woman.

Welcome!

Jean Clayton is a hospital chaplain with a special interest in the grief/healing process. She has worked with support groups and individuals, and has published articles on pastoral care, palliative care and bereavement. She is the mother of four unique young adults and the fortunate grandmother of two-year-old Zachary.

Mary McConnell, our illustrator, has a BFA from Syracuse University and owns, along with her photographer husband Russ, McConnell Studios Ltd. Mary has illustrated four books for Centering and adult literacy math texts for New Readers Press. She and Russ have one son, Sawyer, 2 dogs, 1 cat, 2 froglets and 1 currently-cocooned caterpillar.

This book is dedicated with thanks to all those who have shared their stories and their pain. I dedicate it also with affection to my family, to Yvonne, dearest of friends, and with profound gratitude to Nikki Cordy, most skillful of therapists.

Special Thanks to Centering consultants Rose Jones, Eleanor Hoehne, Beverly Chappell and Louise Vance.

Two beautiful poems appear in this book. *Strawberry Moon* by Mary Oliver is from her book **Twelve Moons** and used with permission from Little, Brown and Company. Our thanks also, to Eileen Moeller for allowing us to use her poem *ten years ago.*

Other Helpful Resources

I Remember, I Remember
   A guided grief journal

The Mourning Handbook
   Practical and generous in affirmation

Companion Through The Darkness
   For young widows

Being A Widow
   Talks about expressing emotion, working with dreams

How To Survive The Loss Of A Love
   A classic and beautifully done

Goodbye My Child
   Loss of children of all ages

Dear Parents
   A support group in print

Inner Healing After Abortion
   Recognizes the grief of pregnancy termination

Why Are The Casseroles Always Tuna?
   Lets some light shine on the sadness

Grief- what it is and what we can do about it.
   Another classic from Centering Corporation

Grieving With Hope
   Every woman will relate to this one

All the above can be ordered from:
Centering Corporation
1531 N Saddle Creek Rd, Omaha NE 68104
Phone: 402-553-1200   Fax: 402-553-0507
EMail: J1200@aol.com